JUGGLING

Step-by-Step

Bobby Besmehn

STERLING INNOVATION
An imprint of Sterling Publishing Co., Inc.

New York / London
www.sterlingpublishing.com

STERLING, the Sterling logo, STERLING INNOVATION, and the Sterling
Innovation logo are registered trademarks of Sterling Publishing Co., Inc.

10 9 8 7 6 5 4 3 2 1

Published in 2009 by Sterling Publishing Co., Inc.
387 Park Avenue South, New York, NY 10016
© 1994 by Sterling Publishing Co., Inc.
Distributed in Canada by Sterling Publishing
C/o Canadian Manda Group, 165 Dufferin Street
Toronto, Ontario, Canada M6K 3H6
Distributed in the United Kingdom by GMC Distribution Services
Castle Place, 166 High Street, Lewes, East Sussex, England BN7 1XU
Distributed in Australia by Capricorn Link (Australia) Pty. Ltd.
P.O. Box 704, Windsor, NSW 2756, Australia

Cover design by Gary Martin

Printed in China
All rights reserved

Sterling ISBN 978-1-4027-6918-4

For information about custom editions, special sales, premium and
corporate purchases, please contact Sterling Special Sales
Department at 800-805-5489 or specialsales@sterlingpublishing.com.

Contents

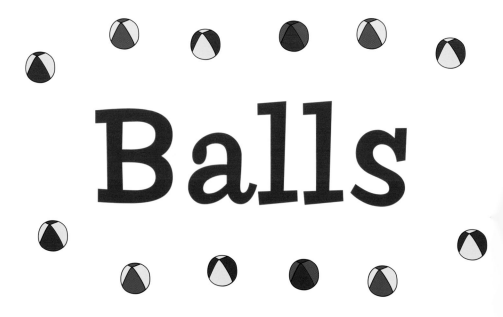

Balls

Step 1 Cascade (One Ball)

Hold the ball cradled in the palm of your dominant hand.

Make a scooping motion from outside to inside as you throw the ball. Release the ball just as it crosses your center line. Catch it in your other hand.

You want the ball to peak about 8 to 10 inches above your head.

Step 2   Cascade (One Ball)

Now go through the same motions starting with your subordinate hand.

Allow the ball to roll from your palm to the middle of your fingers as you release it.

Catch it in your palm.

Your palm should always remain up.

Step 3 Cascade (One Ball)

Keep in mind that balls thrown from the right hand should peak left of your center line—balls thrown from the left hand should peak right of your center line.

Practice this until you can accurately throw the ball from hand to hand, maintaining a steady rhythm. Remember to make a scooping motion with each throw.

Step 1   Cascade (Two Balls)

Cradle one ball in each hand.

You're going to use the same scooping principle for juggling two balls as you did with one.

Toss a ball from your dominant hand. This time, when it reaches the top of its arc or peak, throw the ball in the other hand. It should cross under the first ball and peak at the same height.

Step 2   Cascade (Two Balls)

When the step is complete, the balls should be in opposite hands.

The pictures above show examples of jugging using the scooping motion correctly and incorrectly.

Both balls should remain in the same plane, as in the figure on the left. Otherwise you will either end up chasing the balls or have a much harder time catching them.

Juggling takes place in two dimensions—height and width, not depth.

Step 3   Cascade (Two Balls)

Practice starting with your subordinate hand. If you were throwing right then left, now throw left then right. Practice this until you can do it consistently.

Then try alternating right, left, stop; then left, right, stop; and so on.

You are trying to build a throw, throw-catch, catch rhythm.

Step 1   Cascade (Three Balls)

Start by holding two balls in your dominant hand and one ball in your subordinate hand.

The balls in your dominant hand should be held as such: one ball should be cradled deep within your palm and held in position with your third and fourth fingers. The second ball should be held in front with your thumb, first, and second fingers. This is the first ball thrown.

Step 2   Cascade (Three Balls)

Throw the first ball from your dominant hand. When it reaches its peak, throw the single ball from your other hand.

As soon as this ball reaches it's peak, throw the remaining ball and stop.

Step 3   Cascade (Three Balls)

All balls should be on opposite sides from where they started.

If this worked on the first try, you are doing great. If not, do not get discouraged. With a little more practice, you will find it quite easy. On the next page are a few pointers that might help.

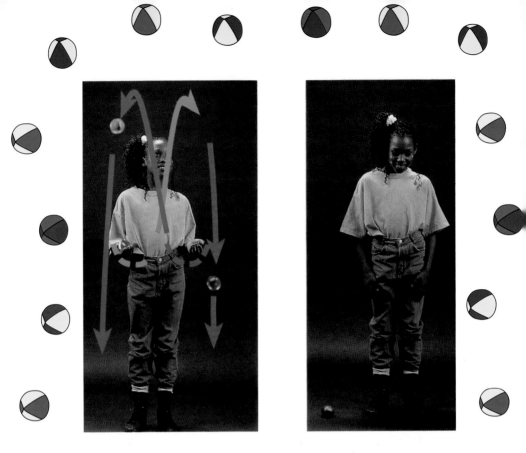

Step 4   Cascade (Three Balls)

If you did not catch all the balls or could not even get them all out in sequence, try the following:

Throw the balls as described, only this time, do not worry about catching them. Just let them fall to the ground.

Your focus should be on when to throw, not how to catch. Each time a ball hits its peak, throw one from the other hand. After landing, the balls should be near your feet on opposite sides from where they began. Work on this for a while, then try to catch them again.

If you got the balls out in sequence, but find yourself chasing them, try this:

Stand facing a wall, an arm's length in front of you. This will help you confine your juggling in the two correct dimensions.

Step 5 Cascade (Three Balls)

Now try starting with your subordinate hand.

Try catching the balls. If you do not, then go through the same steps you went through when you started with your other hand.

After you can throw the balls starting with each hand, move on.

Step 6   Cascade (Three Balls)

Now begin as you did before, starting with your dominant hand. This time, when the third ball reaches its peak, the first ball should be in your subordinate hand. Toss this ball back to your dominant hand and continue throwing a ball every time a ball reaches its peak.

Ball Tricks

Shower (Two Balls in One Hand)

Begin with two balls in your dominant hand. With a scooping motion, throw one ball up, just a little higher than you normally do. Instead of crossing your center line, the ball should shoot right up the side of it.

When the ball reaches its peak, throw the second ball in the same manner.

Now, every time a ball reaches its peak, throw the next one. If you have problems making the balls circle, you might want to try the pattern on the next page.

Columns

The idea is the same as the two-ball shower, except, instead of chasing each other in a circular pattern, the balls are thrown straight up, side by side, and continue to be thrown in this pattern without crossing.

Step 1   The Fake

Now, juggle two balls in either the shower or column pattern while holding a third ball in your subordinate hand.

You should hold the third ball with your fingertips. Your palm should be facing forward as if you are showing it to your audience.

Now, as you juggle, try looking at the third ball. Practice this until it is easy. Doing this may sound silly, but you will find it very helpful for learning this trick.

Step 2 The Fake

Now, rather than simply holding the third ball, you are going to pick one of the two balls you are juggling and track it with the third ball held in your hand.

When you throw the ball you are tracking up, your hand should move up beside it. As the ball comes down, your hand comes down with it.

If you have this timed right, it should take a couple of seconds for your audience to figure out that you are not actually juggling.

The Yo-Yo

To do the Yo-Yo, juggle two balls using the column pattern on page 19. You are going to be tracking a ball as in the fake on pages 20–21, but instead of faking at the side of the ball, you will be above it.

Try imagining a piece of string joining the two balls together and it is your job to keep the string tight. This will create the illusion that the two balls are hooked together.

Clawing

Here is a trick that is quite easy to learn. When performed quickly, it is very flashy.

Instead of juggling with your palms up, juggle with your palms forward.

If you study the picture, you will notice that an outside to inside scooping pattern is still used.

In the beginning, practice with one ball, then two balls, then finally three balls.

Step 1 Behind Your Back

Begin with one ball in your dominant hand.

In one consistent movement, bring the ball around you and throw it over your opposite shoulder, catching it with your subordinate hand.

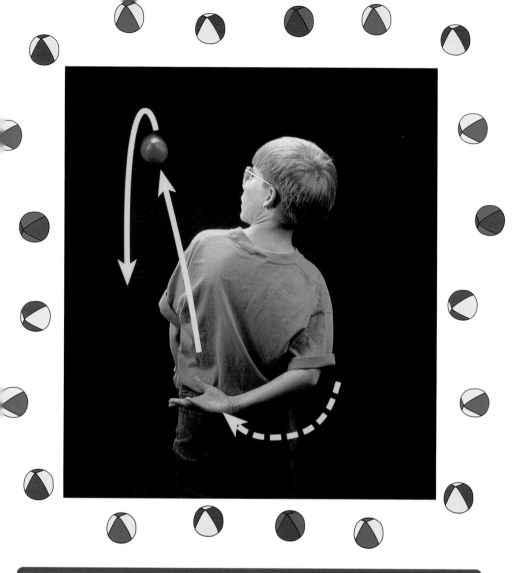

Step 2   Behind Your Back

If you have problems, here are a few ideas you might keep in mind as you practice.

Carry the ball as far around and up your back as possible before releasing it.

Most importantly, before and as you throw, think about catching the ball more than throwing it.

As you gain control, start throwing the ball different heights. Practice throwing with your subordinate hand also.

Step 3 Behind Your Back

Now, try using two balls.

Throw one ball behind your back. When it reaches its peak, throw the other ball in front of you in a cascade pattern.

Practice this until you can do it consistently.

Remember to pause after every second throw. The pause is the place in which the third ball would normally be thrown.

Step 4　Behind Your Back

Now, throw the ball from your subordinate hand first in a cascade. You can throw this ball extra high to allow yourself more time to make the pass behind your back.

If you are doing this correctly, you will not see the ball you are catching with your dominant hand because you are focused on the ball coming around your head.

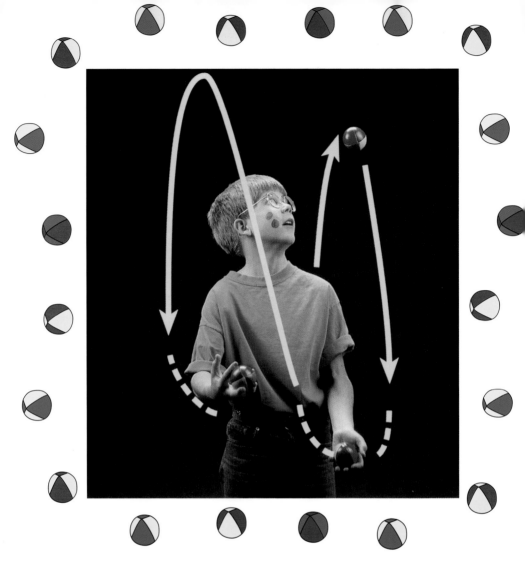

Step 5   Behind Your Back

Now, begin to juggle three balls in a cascade.

Throw a ball from your subordinate hand higher than you normally would. The ball which immediately follows this, thrown from your dominant hand, is the ball which you pass behind your back.

Step 6 Behind Your Back

There is no set height at which you must throw the ball behind your back. You can throw it high or low. As long as you throw it straight up, you will be able to catch it and continue juggling.

As your behind the back throw becomes faster, you will be able to bring the "high ball" down to the height of your regular pattern.

Although this trick may seem difficult at first, with practice, it will become so natural that you do not even think about it. In a short while, you can be doing tricks like "back crosses"—throwing every ball from each hand behind your back. It only takes practice.

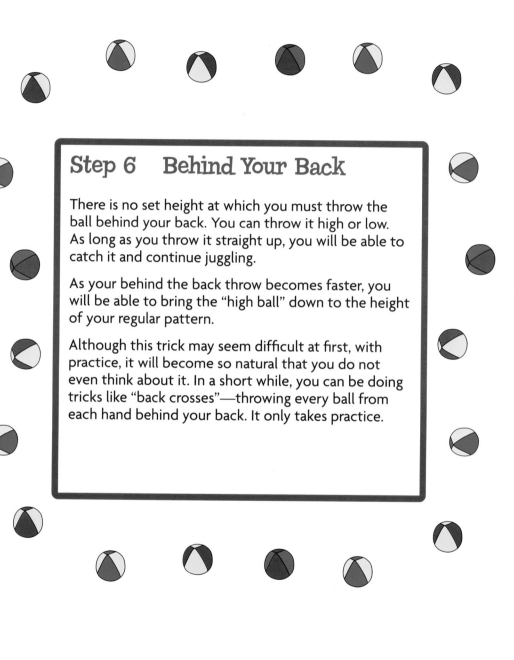

Neck Catch

Throw one ball high. As it falls, bring your upper body down with it. At this point, you should roll your head back and lift your arms, creating a well, with the back of your neck as the bottom. This well is where you catch the ball. Continue moving your upper body downward, stopping gradually as the ball reaches your neck. Do not stop suddenly, or the ball will bounce out.

Other Items

Juggling with Household Items

Rolled-up socks are great for juggling around the house. Tennis balls will work as well. Apples, oranges, and other assorted fruits are fun, but make sure you have permission from your parents when juggling with food.

Step 1   Eating an Apple

To avoid the senseless slaughter of thousands of apples, you should practice these moves with balls before trying it with the apple.

If you can hold a three-ball cascade easily, this trick should come with little effort. It is a classic comedy juggling routine, and, when presented well, it is a trick capable of entertaining any audience.

Step 2　Eating an Apple

Begin juggling three balls in a cascade pattern. Choose one of the balls to represent your apple. When the "apple" ball reaches your dominant hand, throw the ball in your subordinate hand extra high. This gives you time to then kiss the ball that represents the apple and throw it back into the pattern.

Kissing the ball creates the timing and movement you need to take a bite of the actual apple when you use it.

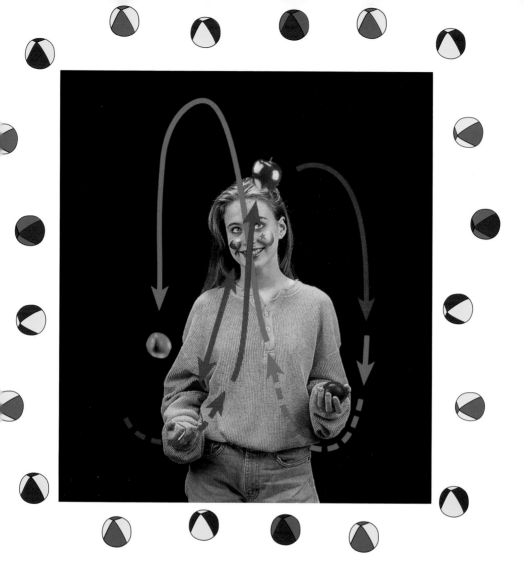

Step 3   Eating an Apple

Remember to catch the highest ball with your dominant hand and toss the "apple" ball to your subordinate hand.

At first, kiss the ball every second or third time it reaches your dominant hand.

Step 4   Eating an Apple

Gradually work toward throwing the highest ball lower and lower, until it is the same height as the rest of the balls in your pattern, and kiss the ball each time it reaches your dominant hand.

If you practice, you will be able to kiss the "apple" ball each time you catch it, using both your subordinate and dominant hands.

Step 5 Eating an Apple (Preparation)

Tips

Remove the stem from the apple and check for worm holes before performing the trick. You do not want any surprises.

Your hands will become sticky as you continue to handle the apple you have bitten into. So whatever else you are juggling with will become sticky as well. Choose balls to juggle that are easy to clean.

Step 6 Eating an Apple (Performance)

When performing, it works well to start as you did when you first learned. Take a bite every second or third time the apple reaches your dominant hand. The first time you take a bite, make it look extremely difficult and act as if you have just done the world's greatest trick. Then, gradually work toward taking a bite each time the apple reaches your dominant hand. Your audience will be amazed and they will probably be falling out of their seats from laughter.

Tricks for Two

Step 1 Two-Person Cascade

Juggling with a friend can be fun! Stand side by side; you can put your arms around each other if you like. (In most cases, this helps in the beginning.)

Practice tossing one ball back and forth. The person on the left uses his or her left hand and the person on the right uses his or her right hand.

Toss the ball the same height as you would for juggling three balls by yourself. Your throws must be accurate for your partner to catch them. And you must both throw the ball the same height to maintain a steady rhythm.

Step 2 Two-Person Cascade

Now, try it with two balls. The person on the right throws first. When the ball reaches its peak, the person on the left throws.

Next, try reversing it. The person on the left throws first. When the ball reaches its peak, the person on the right throws.

Now, try using three balls. You are just doing a cascade pattern, so each time a ball reaches its peak, throw the next one.

Step 3   Two-Person Cascade

If both of you can already juggle, you will find this quite easy!

Bring the pattern down low, then up high, or just see how long you can go!

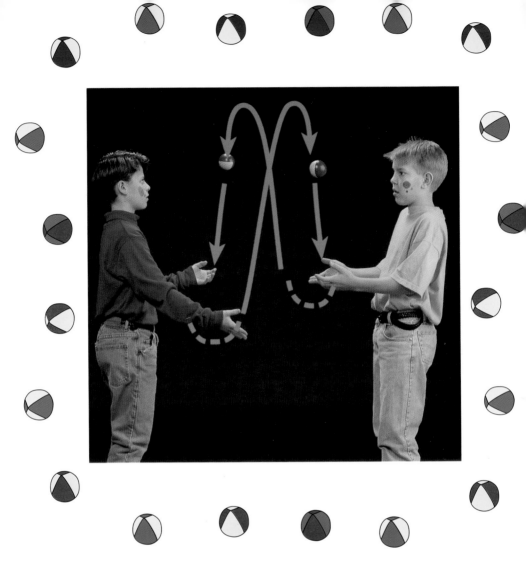

Step 1   Two-Person Pass

To begin, stand facing your partner. Stand about three feet from each other. Each of you holds a ball in your right hand.

Pass the balls straight across, catching them in your left hand. The balls should peak just above eye level.

Now, each of you throws the ball in your left hand to your right hand. Then repeat the steps above.

Step 2   Two-Person Pass

Practicing the moves on this page may help your passing more than anything. You can try it with someone who knows how to juggle or even a friend who does not.

Hold one ball in each hand. Your partner throws you a third ball, as practiced on the previous page. Begin juggling.

Throw the ball from your left hand when the ball your partner throws reaches its peak.

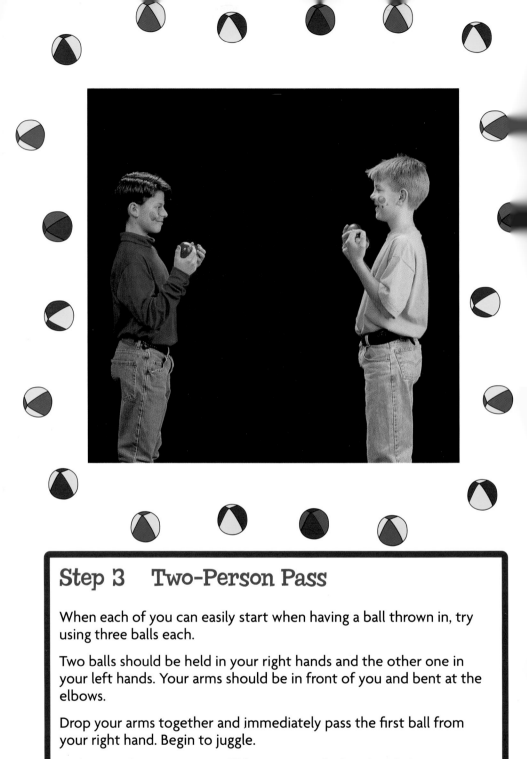

Step 3   Two-Person Pass

When each of you can easily start when having a ball thrown in, try using three balls each.

Two balls should be held in your right hands and the other one in your left hands. Your arms should be in front of you and bent at the elbows.

Drop your arms together and immediately pass the first ball from your right hand. Begin to juggle.

Make two throws to yourself from your right hand and pass again.

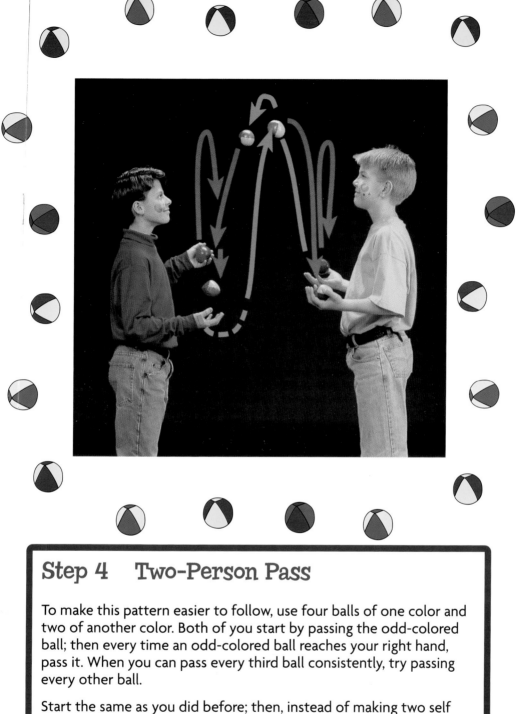

Step 4   Two-Person Pass

To make this pattern easier to follow, use four balls of one color and two of another color. Both of you start by passing the odd-colored ball; then every time an odd-colored ball reaches your right hand, pass it. When you can pass every third ball consistently, try passing every other ball.

Start the same as you did before; then, instead of making two self throws from your right hand, only make one.

The pattern goes pass, self throw, pass, self throw, pass, and so on. The red arrows show the height at which your self throws should peak.

Step 5   Two-Person Pass

This next pattern takes a little more practice, but most can learn it in a week or less.

Warm up by practicing the patterns on the previous pages.

Now, start with a pass; then, every time a ball reaches your right hand, pass it.

Glossary

Ball: A round object used in juggling. Usually made of rubber.

Cascade: Basic juggling pattern in which objects thrown from your right hand peak left of your center line, and objects thrown from your left hand peak right of your center line.

Center Line: An imaginary line which runs up the center of your body. It connects with the ground and stretches high over your head.

Dominant Hand: The hand you eat with, write with, and generally use the most.

Peak: The highest point an object reaches when it is thrown.

Self-Throw: A term used mostly when passing. It represents the throws to yourself from the passing hand.

Subordinate Hand: The hand which you use the least.

Index